ICG Masquerade Guidelines

About the International Costumers' Guild Press

The International Costumers' Guild Press is the publication arm of the non-profit International Costumers' Guild (ICG). Its mission is to publish long-form content including books and monographs on topics related to costumes and costuming.

The ICG is an affiliation of hobbyist and professional costumers, dedicated to the promotion and education of costuming, including cosplay, as an art form in all its aspects. The ICG Press serves the ICG's mission as a non-profit educational organization.

For more information about the ICG and to locate a chapter near you, visit its website: *https://www.costume.org*.

If you have an idea for a book or a manuscript that is ready for publication, contact the Editor in Chief at *icgpress-editor@costume.org*.

International Costumers'
Guild Press

ICG Masquerade Guidelines

2021 Edition

International Costumers' Guild

These Guidelines assist costume Masquerade Directors in writing and implementing rules to ensure fair competition in the Masquerades they run, and provide a resource for ensuring that all aspects of a successful Masquerade are covered.

Produced in the United States of America.
Publication Date: January 2025.
Publisher: International Costumers' Guild Press.
Cover Design: Philip J. Gust.
Cover Art: JLG via Pixabay.
(*https://pixabay.com/illustrations/background-scrapbooking-paper-1988369/*)

ISBN 978-1-966384-00-7 (Softcover)
ISBN 978-1-966384-01-4 (Hardcover)
ISBN 978-1-966384-02-1 (eBook)

Library of Congress Control Number: 2024951778

"…more what you'd call 'guidelines'
than actual rules."

Captain Barbossa, *Pirates of the Caribbean*

CONTENTS

Mission

The members of the International Costumers' Guild, Inc. (ICG) have developed these Masquerade Guidelines to promote fairness and equity in Masquerade competition and judging. The ICG Guidelines are rooted in decades of our members' experience as costumed participants, judges, producers, and directors of such competitions. We hope these Guidelines will help make both novice and accomplished costumers' experiences with Masquerade competition and costuming more comfortable and enjoyable.

Context

The purpose of these Guidelines is to assist Masquerade Directors in writing and implementing rules to ensure fair competition in the Masquerades they run, and to provide a resource for ensuring that all aspects of a successful Masquerade are covered. These Guidelines have been developed to serve international[*] Masquerade competitions, but they may be adapted and applied when writing rules for any costume competition at any convention.

While Masquerade Directors are our intended primary audience, any participant (costumer, crew member, or judge) in any Masquerade can benefit from reviewing these Guidelines.

Revision History

These Guidelines began with the ICG's formal ratification of what we now call the Skill Division System, which Peggy Kennedy first debuted at the 1981 Denver World Science Fiction Convention. The Division System was originally designed to encourage fairer competition amongst a field of entries of widely varying skill and experience, as were the resulting ICG Guidelines. The first version of these ICG Guidelines was adopted May 24, 1992 and was subsequently amended February 21, 1994, May 26, 2006, and January 20, 2010.

---

[*] Any competition that draws both entrants and audience from outside the host country can be considered an international competition. (See the section on Scope of Competition.)

In the intervening years, members of the ICG have gained additional experience in running, judging, and entering Masquerades, and this revision is intended to incorporate "best practices" based on that experience.

This revision, adopted on April 25, 2021, is intended to be a living document, reflecting members' continuing experience with the art of Masquerade Costuming (as recognized by the Library of Congress and other national collections) in all its forms.

Inquiries

Inquiries or concerns about and suggestions for modifications to the Guidelines may be directed to *guidelines@costume.org*. Your input is valued; your correspondence will be referred to the appropriate members of the Guidelines committee for review and consideration.

Terms

Competition names may vary by event and venue (including names such as "Cosplay Competition" and "Costume Contest"). For consistency's sake, in these Guidelines we will refer to all staged competitions as "Masquerades."

Masquerade

A Masquerade is a staged show where costume entries are presented before an audience and a panel of judges. These presentations may take the form of fashion walks or short time-limited theatrical vignettes. The judges deliberate and then announce awards for the winning entries. Awards may be made for a variety of criteria.

As described in these Guidelines, it is expected that most of the costume entrants in a Masquerade are amateurs, hobbyists, or other enthusiasts of varying skill levels rather than professional costumers.

Masquerade Director

The Masquerade Director is the person or persons in charge of the competition.

Master of Ceremonies

The Master of Ceremonies (MC) is the public face of the Masquerade during the event; some Masquerade Directors may prefer to use the term Host, Announcer, or some other term for this role. The MC is responsible for managing the smooth flow of the Masquerade in real time on-site during the show itself, announcing each entry in turn to the audience, making any necessary other announcements, and filling time with banter if there must be a delay before proceeding with an entry.

The Masquerade Director may also choose to have the Awards announced by the MC once the judges' deliberations are complete.

Some Masquerade Directors serve this role as well as the backstage management during the Masquerade. Others may choose an additional party as MC to present the event, working in combination with the Masquerade Director and Technical Director/Stage Manager.

Awards/Judging Categories

Most Masquerades announce awards for Presentation, based on how the costumes appear when presented on stage, and Workmanship, based on close examination of the costumes backstage.

Awards for Research and/or Documentation may also be appropriate, particularly for historical and culturally significant costumes, or for visual media-based reproductions.

Some Masquerades also make awards for theatrical components of the presentation itself, such as choreography.

Costume

A Costume is an ensemble of clothing, accessories, props, and wearable art that is. typically, not everyday street wear for the person wearing them on stage, or for the audience viewing them.[*] The Director may specify what types of costumes are appropriate for their Masquerade.

Original vs Re-creation Costumes

Costumes may be original designs, or re-creations -- of an extant costume, or one represented in one of the visual arts.

Note that creating a costume based on a textual description with no visual representation is considered an original design based on or inspired by a literary work, not a re-creation, as there is no visual reference to re-create.

Methods of Costume Creation

Costumes may be created in a variety of ways:

- Constructed from raw materials by any number of techniques including sewing. Constructed costumes are usually eligible for both workmanship and presentation awards.
- Modified from extant objects and garments. Modified costumes are usually eligible for both workmanship and presentation awards, depending on the degree of modification.
- Assembled from "found" or purchased items, where no craftsmanship/construction was involved. Assembled Costumes are usually eligible for Presentation awards, but not for Workmanship.

---

[*] This is a deliberately vague generalization. What constitutes a costume for a competition essentially comes down to what the Director accepts as an entry.

- Purchased or Commissioned costumes are purchased outright by the wearer. These costumes are typically not eligible for awards, but may be included in the show as Exhibition Only entries.

Note: A constructed costume made by someone other than the person presenting it on stage may still qualify for competition if the maker is also present at the event and credited as part of the entry. The maker's skills and experience should be considered when selecting the appropriate Skill Division for the entry.

The Masquerade Director may choose to make exceptions for costumes constructed by family members, especially in the case of Youth entrants.

Alternatively, if a Masquerade is part of an event which offers limited or supporting (non-attending) memberships, the Director may elect to only require that the maker have that more limited membership to qualify a costume for entry.

The Masquerade Director ultimately determines which costumes are allowed in their Masquerade.

Documentation

Documentation is reference material (physical or electronic) that the costumer provides to judges that explain aspects of their entry which may not be immediately apparent on visual inspection. Most often required for re-creation costumes, documentation serves as a visual reference to an existing artwork or garment.

Documentation may be as simple as copies of photos or artwork that illustrate the source of the costume design, whether for re-creation or as inspiration.

Documentation may also demonstrate the research done while designing/creating/assembling the costume, or to explain the techniques used in its creation.

The Masquerade Director determines the requirements and any limits on documentation for their masquerade, which should be clearly stated in the rules.

Registration

Registration is the process by which costumers enter a masquerade. It may be as simple as a paper signup sheet, or as elaborate as an online form and database system. The Masquerade Director determines the process they will use for their event.

General Respect for Participants

Anyone interacting directly with costumers should do so in a fair and considerate manner. It's not unusual for costumers to be held in close quarters during the Masquerade process, so respecting personal space and awareness of a person's comfort should always be paramount. Err on the side of caution when working in the Masquerade environment.

Always ask for permission before getting up close or touching a costumer and/or costume.

This attitude of mutual respect should be encouraged generally, for crew, judges, staff, and all participants.

The ICG encourages the implementation of a robust and well-thought-out Code of Conduct for events as one means to encourage respectful behavior.

The Masquerade Director's Role

The Masquerade Director Is in Charge

In any Masquerade, the Director's word is law. Their rules and judgement calls set the tone for the entire Masquerade. A Masquerade Director should be considerate and fair in their interactions with staff and entrants. An important step in this direction is to write down all Masquerade rules and make them available to all entrants and staff members before the event, on the event website and/or through social media, as well as in hard copy at the event.

Creating Rules

These Guidelines can form the basis of a fair and equitable set of Masquerade rules. Many of these Guidelines (such as the definition of "professional costumer") are intentionally vague. A Masquerade Director should cultivate a sense of good judgment and fairness when developing and applying their particular event's rules. We encourage Directors to adapt and interpret these Guidelines in the manner that best fits their venue, participants, and community.

Implementing Skill Divisions

If the competition is using Skill Divisions to split the field of entrants, the Masquerade Director is the ultimate arbiter of who enters in which Division. This includes assisting entrants with selecting the appropriate Division for themselves, and handling questions from the judges if they believe an entrant has entered in an inappropriate Division.

Ensuring Fair Judging

A fair competition requires respectable and impartial judges. The Masquerade Director must take care when selecting judges to ensure they are knowledgeable in the field and have appropriate skills to judge craftsmanship and performance aspects. The Director should write instructions for judges and include them in the published rules. This is an important step in establishing a standard of impartiality and transparency.

While judging systems vary, it is good practice to state the judging system being used in an event. For example, if a Masquerade will use a points system, the categories for which points will be awarded and total number of possible points should be standard across all Skill Divisions.

Good judges bring their experience and opinions to the table. Judges should be given the freedom to recognize excellence and achievement in the way they see fit. In general, the Masquerade Director should not mandate award names and quotas, but should leave these decisions to the judges' discretion. (There may, however, be special awards with specific criteria as determined by the Masquerade Director, the convention, or sponsors.)

The Judges' Role

So, You've Been Asked to Judge a Masquerade. Now What?

Judging a Masquerade is, at minimum, a commitment of at least a few hours during an evening at a convention. On the plus side, judges will see all Masquerade entries from the best possible vantage point. On the minus side, the deliberation process can go quite late, especially if there is a large entry count. It is not unusual for Masquerade Directors to thank judges for this extended commitment by providing amenities such as snacks, water, or food, (especially if the judging process lasts all day, as with a Costume-Con Historical Masquerade).

Workmanship judges have the task of selecting aspects of a costume entry that might be worth noting above other entries, for choice of material, skill of construction or embellishment, or for any other reason. Presentation judges view the complete costume and how it moves or changes across the stage during the Masquerade.

Ideally, Workmanship judges will also have the opportunity to view costumes as they are presented on stage during the Masquerade.

This commitment is to be taken seriously. Most Masquerade entrants have invested time, materials, the cost of travel, and many hours of work to display their artworks. It is the responsibility of the judges' panel to award that work in appropriate ways. The following recommendations are specifically addressed to judges, whether new or with years of experience.

Each Competition is Unique
Judges should base their opinion of an entry only on what they see on stage or in the workmanship judging area during the Masquerade. Other influences, including comments from the MC, should be disregarded. (If, however, an entry evokes a particularly strong response from the audience on its own merit, that is worth noting by a presentation judge.)

Performance of an entrant or entry in past competitions should not affect judges' consideration in the event at hand, unless it is directly relevant to the rules of the current competition. Such concerns should be raised with the Masquerade Director.

Judge the Field of Entries Before You
Judging should be based on the quality of entries' technical workmanship and stage presentation.

Replay/Reset of an Entry
If an entry is replayed due to technical problems or crew error, judges should do their best to disregard the first appearance.

Bias/Conflict of Interest
We recognize that judges selected from the community frequently know and have relationships with entrants who may appear before them.

Judges are expected to avoid conflicts of interest. Judges should inform the Masquerade Director if they may be influenced by a personal or business relationship. This is known as a bias or nepotism clause, and can be exercised by the judge, or required by the Masquerade Director if they know about the relationship prior to judging.

In the event of such a conflict, it is the Masquerade Director's responsibility to consult with the judging panel to find an appropriate solution. Solutions may include a judge's recusal from deliberations where the costumer in question is involved, retiring from the judging panel, or being removed entirely. In a situation requiring that a judge be removed from the panel, replacing the judge, or continuing the Masquerade with fewer judges is at the Masquerade Director's discretion.

Deliberation, Not Discrimination

Masquerade costuming as we practice it is an inclusive art and art is open to interpretation. Judges should be impartial. Discrimination based on race, color, creed, disability, gender, gender identity, sexual orientation, ethnicity, body type, (either regarding the costumer *or* the costumed character) or for any other reason is a detriment to the Masquerade's inclusive environment. Abuse stifles interpretation, creates a toxic environment, and should not be tolerated or permitted. In the case of protected classes, such as those listed above, there may be legal ramifications as well.

We recommend that a zero-tolerance policy for such discrimination be communicated to Masquerade staff, judges, and participants.

Practice Unimpaired Judging

If a judge is found to be incapacitated due to illness, inebriation, or intoxication, the Masquerade Director should retire or remove the judge from the panel.

Practice Respectful Judging

When interacting directly with costumers (whether in-person during workmanship judging or after the competition), judges, like Masquerade Directors, are asked to be fair and considerate.

Workmanship Judges must take care when inspecting a costumer's work. Always ask for permission before getting up close or touching a costumer or costume.

Be Prepared to Move to the Entry for Workmanship Judging

Large costumes, or costumes with limited mobility/visibility, may have difficulty coming to a workmanship judging area. Accommodate those entries by moving to them where they have been placed.

The Masquerade Director may opt to have Workmanship judges move through the Green Room rather than designate a judging area.

Special Considerations for Judging

Costume Re-creation

Some Masquerade competitions and venues lend themselves to or actively promote the re-creation of costumes from media and art. Sources may include but are not by any means limited to costumes depicted in television or film (whether live-action or animated), two-dimensional art (illustrations, cover-art, or photographs), or three-dimensional art (sculpture, existing garments, or even such esoteric sources as toys).

Judges are not expected to recognize every re-creation costume and source. Entrants should be encouraged to provide documentation showing or describing the costumes they are re-creating, to aid the judges in evaluating the merits of their entries. (See the Documentation section below.)

Because costume re-creation can draw on skills that differ from those used when creating original designs, judges should consider offering separate competitive awards for re-creation and original designs.

Historical Competitions
There are several ways in which historical competition is different from the Masquerades presented at science fiction, fantasy, anime, and other media-focused conventions. The recommendations described in this section are based on current practices for the Costume-Con Historical Masquerade.

All entries in a historical competition are expected to have a basis in period costume or design; documentation that supports an entry's historical origin is suggested or may be required in the Masquerade rules for all entries. (See the Documentation section below.)

To help the judges evaluate each entry on its own merit, entries may be categorized as either Historical Re-creation (i.e. a faithful reproduction of a period garment) or Historical Interpretation (i.e. a design based on a period garment or style that may intentionally depart from the style of the period).

Re-creation and Interpretation categories may be judged separately at the discretion of the Masquerade Director.

Judging criteria are often very different in historical competitions. An entrant's Skill Division placement in historical competition is not directly linked to their placement in other Masquerades. For example, a costumer may enter in the Novice Division in the Historical Masquerade at a Costume-Con and in the Journeyman Division elsewhere. As always, placement is at the discretion of the Masquerade Director.

Historical re-creation and living history organizations often grant awards for costuming. These awards may be weighed in considering Skill Division placement (again, at the discretion of the costumer and the Masquerade Director).

Other organizations offer their own international awards. International historical costume awards (for example, the SCA's Laurel in Costuming) should definitely be considered in placement. It is suggested that when entering a historical competition, the recipient of such an international award compete in the Master Division.

Technical Workmanship

Masquerade entries often include a wide variety of workmanship techniques, including but not limited to sewing, armor crafting, 3D printing, electronic fabrication, and embellishment of all sorts. Judges should be aware that bigger and flashier does not always mean better and more impressive, nor does the use of more advanced and niche technological advancements give a costumer an unfair advantage. Every technique presents its own unique challenges and each entry should be judged by how well those challenges are met.

For example, a fabric arts-based costume may be judged by the quality of seam finishing, lining technique, and pattern drafting or alterations, while a 3D printed prop can be judged by the print quality, layer smoothing and finishing techniques, and whether or not the entrant did their own digital 3D modeling design.

With the constant advancement in technology and its use in costuming, it is not unusual to come across costumes made with materials or techniques with which a judge may be unfamiliar. It is good practice to select judges who specialize in different areas of costuming so that they can field questions from other judges regarding the nature of the materials used.

For example, a judge whose primary focus is fiber arts may not be familiar with thermoplastics or foam crafting, whereas an armor crafter may have little knowledge of fiber arts but be well versed in metal work, chainmail, and other armor styles including thermoplastics and foam. It is essential to ensure that judging remains fair and unbiased regarding workmanship, no matter whether the judge is familiar with the material and technique or not. When in doubt, judges should base awards on the workmanship and appearance or presentation of the costume as appropriate.

Workmanship Judges are encouraged to offer major and competitive awards such as Best Armor or Best Seamster in Division as best fit the entries. (See the section on Awards and Award Naming.)

Large Costumes

A large costume is defined as a costume that exceeds or extends past the size of the costumer's normal body. Large costumes include designs such as form-fitted costumes with wings, a large suit of foam or thermoplastic armor, a mechanized battle mech or robot, or an immense dragon with puppetry. The Masquerade Director will need to make careful logistical decisions before the Masquerade and take potential risks, navigation, staging, and judging requirements into careful consideration.

Judging of large costumes can be a daunting task; however, it is essential that all costumes be considered on their own individual merits and awarded appropriately. It is imperative that judges take care to weigh the merits of large costumes as they would with costumes made in any other method or specialty.

Documentation

Documentation Requirements
Appropriate documentation can help the judges understand the nature of an entry and influence the judges' decisions. Entrants should always be encouraged to provide documentation for the judges.

Documentation may be as simple as a single reference photo, a more complete packet of references and progress photos, or even a thesis project providing justification and documentation for each creative decision along the way.

It is the Masquerade Director's responsibility to ensure that any submitted documentation is given to the judging panels. To provide a level playing field, it is best to specify in the rules the minimum required documentation and maximum recommended documentation, as well as the number of copies required for an entry.

Research and Documentation Awards
It is appropriate for a judge to verify documentation and references, especially those involving costumes from a fandom, culture, or other category with which they are not familiar.

For example, if a judge is unfamiliar with the character that the entrant is portraying, it is acceptable to ask for documentation that may not have been provided, including a photo or visual reference, and it is appropriate for judges to use their own electronic devices to find reference to that character or check citations. They should, however, make absolutely certain any such searches yield correct references (For example: are they looking up the correct incarnation of Doctor Who – which has had over a dozen different actors portray the character?)

Judges must take great care to do the due diligence required to ensure that documentation is carefully reviewed and awarded on its merits.

Costumers presenting large costumes should be encouraged to provide documentation of their fabrication process, including samples of materials so that the judges can accurately form an opinion on the workmanship aspects.

The Masquerade Director may specify that general awards for Research and/or Documentation will be made; in that event, an awards policy like that for workmanship and presentation judging should be implemented. Note that this may entail additional judges or separate judging time from the on-stage competition.

Even in the absence of general documentation awards, Judges may offer special awards for research and documentation as they see fit.

Awards and Award Naming

General Award Philosophy
A consistent award scheme is essential in promoting fairness and equity between different competitions. "Excellence deserves recognition" should be the guiding principle for any judging panel: If an entry shows merit, the costumer(s) should receive an award.

We recommend *not* having pre-set awards or award quotas for the judging panels (with the exception of special themed or sponsored awards).

In our experience, a rough target where no more than half of the entries receive recognition, including minor awards, works well for most competitions. This is not, however, a hard and fast benchmark.

If a Masquerade has a small contingent of Youth or Young Fan entries, there is a tradition of recognizing all those entries with at least an Honorable Mention award, in the interest of encouraging enthusiasm for entering future competitions. There absolutely can be Competitive and Major awards in the Youth Division, and entries from that Division can and should be considered eligible for Best in Show if they merit such consideration.

Division Reassignment
A competition may have a significantly larger number of entries in a single Skill Division, or perhaps a Division with only a single entry.

Judges may not arbitrarily assign an entry to a higher or lower Skill Division to "even out" the Divisions; any such reassignments should only be made by the Masquerade Director.

Rather than arbitrarily "bumping" entries to a higher Skill Division, the judges and Director should consider being more generous with awards in the large Division.

Judges might also suggest to the Masquerade Director that a single-entry division be collapsed together with another Division.

Classes of Awards

The ICG recommends three classes of awards: Competitive Awards (within one or across Divisions), and Major and Minor Awards within each Skill Division, and a standard naming convention for such awards to make it easier for costumers to choose their Skill Division in future competitions. Whether an entry is given an award is at the discretion of the judging panel.

Competitive Awards

Competitive Awards using such titles as "Best in Division" and "Best in Show" are the only awards given to one entry relative to other entries. These awards have the greatest weight when considering an entrant's Skill Division placement.

Judges should not be obliged to present a competitive award if there is no consensus on a winner. For instance: if they cannot agree on Best in Show, they may state so and decline to specify one. If there is only a single entry in a Skill Division, they may decline to award Best in Division, as there are no entries to compare for that Division.

Major awards

Major Awards do affect future Skill Division placement. We suggest that judging panels use "Best [Descriptor]," "Award for [Descriptor]" or "Excellence in/for [Descriptor]," to clearly identify major awards.

Judge's Choice or Judges' Choice may be used as a major award name to recognize an entry without calling out specific characteristics of the costume.

Note: It is generally advised to avoid using a "Best" or "Most" descriptor if the entry is the only one of its type. For example: instead of a "Best Historical Dress" award when there is only a single Historical Dress entry, the award would be better acknowledged as "Excellence in Historical Dress.

Minor Awards

Minor Awards need not be considered for Skill Division placement.

We suggest that judging panels use "Honorable Mention" as part of their name to clearly identify minor awards.

Humor in Award Names

There is a tradition of wordplay in the naming of Masquerade awards, particularly in the case of particularly humorous or evocative entries. We support that tradition, with the proviso that the name also makes clear the nature of the award.

In other words, a serious award with a humorous title is still an award, but an award should not be made as a joke and especially not at the expense of the entrant (or others).

Prizes and Award Presentation

Awards vs Prizes

Awards are the recognition of excellence that the judging panel makes for the field of entries in a Masquerade.

Prizes are whatever physical or monetary acknowledgement a Masquerade presents as a token of that recognition.

Prizes can be as simple as a certificate, ribbon, or trophy. Sometimes they may be items of significant value, whether services, goods, memberships, gift certificates or even money.

A sponsored "special award for xxx" with a prize is generally a reasonable request from its sponsor. A restriction barring possible awards for something in return for funding a competitive cash prize (for instance "no Best Sailor Moon award") is more problematic. It's important that the value of prizes not derange the judging process.

Budgetary constraints may limit the number of trophies, ribbons, or other tokens available for prizes. If there are insufficient tokens for all awards, we recommend assigning them to award winners hierarchically, starting with Competitive Awards, then working down through Major and then Minor awards. (For instance, if there are not enough award ribbons for all winners, give them to the "Best in Show" and "Best in Division" entries, then to the Major Award winners.)

Presentation of Awards

It is preferable to announce award results in front of the audience. If possible, each award recipient should be brought back on stage to be acknowledged and presented with the token, if any, of their award.

If time and/or space limitations prevent this, we suggest that:

- Competitive and Major Awards should be given on stage during the awards ceremony and acknowledged with a certificate, trophy, ribbon or other token, in-kind prize goods, or monetary remuneration.

- Minor awards be acknowledged on stage during the awards ceremony, with or without a certificate or other token.
- Certificates, if desired, should be created for all awards. This may not be possible within the time constraints of the Masquerade itself. If it isn't possible to deliver the certificates with the awards immediately after the Masquerade, arrange for entrants to collect them the next day, or send them to entrants once they are created and signed.
- If a Masquerade includes any particularly young entrants, it is wise to arrange for quick judging of those entries and announcement of any awards earlier in the evening, so that the youngest entrants and their parents/guardians can leave for an earlier bedtime.

Scope of Competition

Masquerades draw a wide variety of entrants. The ICG recognizes four general scopes of competition, based on the geographical range from which they draw. To help determine a costumer's appropriate Skill Division, the scope of each competition may be taken into consideration when weighing the awards a costumer has received in previous competitions.

Local
Local events may be hosted by libraries, clubs, or conventions with attendees and entrants from a narrow area.

Regional
Costumers and audience members come from the wider region or multiple metropolitan areas participate in the convention.

National
Large events which draw participants and audience from around the country.

International
Any event that draws both entrants and audience from around the country and outside the host country.

Masquerade Directors may determine the scope of their competition based on their attendees and entrants, and advertise the scope as they see fit.

ICG Accredited International Competitions

ICG Accredited International Competitions are International-scope competitions which the ICG has determined are peer events, not only in the range and skill of entries they garner, but in their technical quality of production and entrant support. As of 1 January, 2020, three conventions had their Masquerades so accredited: WorldCon, Costume-Con, and Anime North.

The original version of these Guidelines was developed with those competitions in mind.

More information on this policy is available at *https://www.costume.org/wp/standards-of-practice-for-costume-competitions-requesting-icg-recognition-as-international/*

Reason for Skill Divisions

Competition with one's peers is the cornerstone of fairness. We believe it is unreasonable for someone new to Masquerade costuming to compete for every award against costumers with years of Masquerade experience.

The ICG recommends a skill- and experience-based division of Masquerade entrants into competition groups (Skill Divisions) to ensure that both novice and experienced costumers have a reasonably equal chance to win the Major and Competitive awards given in Masquerades.

The Skill Division System is not intended to provide recognition; the awards themselves do that. The Division System exists merely to promote fairness. Outside of any single competition, Skill Division ranking is meaningless.

Once again: Skill Divisions are intended to make each competition fairer; they are not an earned rank system administered by any authority.

The ICG has chosen a three-tier Skill Division system for large international competitions. If a competition is smaller or draws a narrower range of skills and experience, the Skill Division system may be adapted as appropriate. At one time, the ICG suggested an additional level between the middle and top Skill Divisions; that level was eliminated in the 2006 revision of these Guidelines.

For historical reasons, these Skill Divisions are referred to as Novice, Journeyman, and Master. To avoid confusion with the classifications used by professional Costumers Unions, some Masquerade Directors prefer to use terms such as Beginner-Intermediate-Experienced, Novice-Intermediate-Open, or variations thereof instead.

The Basics

The Novice Division exists to encourage people who are new to costuming and Masquerades to compete.

The Journeyman Division is an intermediate Division for costumers who have consistently won awards in the Novice Division, but who feel they are not yet ready to compete in the Master Division.

The Master Division is open to any costumer who wishes to enter.

It is considered good practice for Masquerade Directors to require anyone who is a known professional in the field, or has had exceptional success in past Masquerades, to enter as a Master in competition.

The ICG has also defined a Junior/Youth Division so young costumers who participate in the design and construction of their own costumes need not compete against adults unless they wish to.

The ICG has not defined a fixed age range for competition in a Junior/Youth Division, as such a determination should be at the discretion of the Masquerade Director. In some Masquerades, it is commonly accepted that a person who has not yet reached the age of majority would be considered in such a category unless they wish to compete in any higher category; however, in most ICG-style Masquerades, the age limit is 13, because that is the age at which an ICG member may vote on ICG-related business.

For many Masquerades, a simple two-tier system comprised of "Novice" and "Experienced" can be adequate and fair. Again, each Masquerade Director should consider what is most appropriate to their Masquerade.

Determining a Costumer's Placement in the Division System

The Skill Divisions are designed to protect less experienced entrants from being forced into competition against more experienced costumers before they are ready. Each Division is defined in terms of restrictions.

As there is no committee or organization that tracks all costumers' wins for placement purposes, an entrant's placement in any Division is based on a combination of the honor system and the Masquerade Director's discretion.

As mentioned above, the scope of each competition may be taken into consideration when weighing the awards a costumer has received in previous competitions.

We offer the following suggested restrictions on who may *not* enter in each Division:

Master
- Any costumer may enter in the Master Division.
- This is the Division where professional costumers should compete.

Journeyman

- Professional costumers may not enter in the Journeyman Division.
- An entrant who has competed and won in the Master Division in a competition of equal or larger scope may not enter in the Journeyman Division.
- An entrant who has won "Best in Show" or "Best Journeyman" in a competition of equal or larger scope may not enter in the Journeyman Division. and should compete in the Master Division.
- An entrant who has won more than three major awards in the Journeyman Division in a competition of equal or larger scope may not enter in the Journeyman Division.
- Awards won at competitions of smaller scope may be counted towards Division placement at the discretion of the costumer and the Masquerade Director.
- Minor awards may be counted towards placement at the discretion of the costumer.

Novice

- Professional costumers may not enter in the Novice Division.
- An entrant who has competed and won in any Division other than Novice in a competition of equal or larger scope may not enter in the Novice Division.
- An entrant who has won a Competitive Award (Best in Show, Best in Division) in a competition of equal or larger scope may not enter in the Novice Division.
- An entrant who has won numerous major awards in the Novice Division in competitions of similar scope is encouraged to enter in the Journeyman Division.
- Awards won at competitions of smaller scope may be counted towards Division placement at the discretion of the costumer and the Masquerade Director.
- Minor awards may be counted towards placement at the discretion of the costumer.

Competing Up and Other Considerations

Costumers may always choose to compete in a higher (less restricted) Division than their previous awards indicate or in which the Masquerade Director has placed them. They may not choose to compete in a lower (more restricted) Division.

Major awards given in jest are only counted at the discretion of the costumer. Such awards should be counted if the presentation in question was intentionally comic.

If a costumer has won multiple awards for the same entry, only the highest award should be considered towards placement (see Judging Guidelines). For example, if all awards from multiple Masquerades won by an entry are minor awards, the entrant should count one minor award. If they have won multiple major awards for that entry, the entrant should count one major award. The next section (on Entering a Costume in Multiple Competitions) discusses some other important considerations on a costume which has received multiple awards.

Entering a Costume in Multiple Competitions

It is considered unsporting to enter a costume that has won a major award in a larger Masquerade with relatively stiff competition at a smaller Masquerade with less competition in the same Skill Division. Fairness concerns about repeat entries may be offset if the costumer is willing to enter the costume in a more experienced Skill Division.

Costumes may be entered in more than one competition under the following circumstances:

- A costume that has not won an award in competition may be entered in another Masquerade.
- A costume that has won a major award may be entered again in a competition of similar size at the discretion of the Masquerade Director (usually if the audience, judges, and slate of entries are significantly different).
- A costume that has won a major award in competition may be entered again in a larger competition.
- A costume that has won a major award in competition may be entered again in a higher Skill Division.
- A costume that has won a major award in competition may be entered in exhibition (not judged in competition).

A costume that has won a **Competitive Award** (such as Best in Show or Best in Division) in an international-scope competition *should not* be entered in competition at any other Masquerade. (See Judging Guidelines.)

If the Masquerade Director determines it would not be fair to enter a costume in competition in any Skill Division, we recommend the Director consider encouraging the entrant to show the costume in exhibition (not judged in competition).

Essential Timeline of a Masquerade

The basic sequence of events for a Masquerade proceeds something like this (dramatically simplified).

Well Before the Event
- Event is planned and announced (date, time, and location)
- Rules are announced
- Judges are selected
- Technical requirements are submitted to the hosting event and announced (if possible)

Entry signups may begin
- Shortly before the event (same or previous day)
- Entry signups continue and then close
- Rehearsals, if any, take place
- Run order of the entries is determined

The show itself
- Entries assemble
- Entries are put in order
- Final review of entry requirements (script, etc.)
- Backstage workmanship judging takes place
- Audience is seated for the show
- CURTAIN! (the show begins)
- Entries are presented to the audience
- Judges retire to deliberate
- (Something takes place to entertain the audience while the judges deliberate)
- Judges return
- Awards are announced

After the show
- Complete list of entries and all award winners is compiled and published (preferably with photos)
- Any remaining certificates or prizes are prepared and delivered to entrants

- Archival material (photos/video/etc.) is prepared and delivered to the hosting event, the ICG Archivist, and any other individuals who should receive the material.

Facilities

Stage Design
The Masquerade Director is responsible for providing entrants with quality technical support. They should publish what technical aspects and amenities are available to entrants, as well as stage dimensions and accessibility accommodations as soon as possible. It is good practice to provide these details and, when available, a diagram of the stage layout, on the event website and social media as applicable.

Safety
Stage design should consider the safety of entrants, staff, crew, and audience.

Masquerade Directors should remember that most entrants are amateur performers, and many will likely be both nervous and unfamiliar with backstage practices. Large costumes present additional challenges to planning for safety: Costumers with large costumes should contact the Masquerade Director in advance to discuss their needs and possible accommodations (including storage and any mobility issues) so that reasonable efforts can be made to ensure the safety of the costumer, Masquerade staff, other entrants, and spectators.

- Walkways should be clear of obstruction.
- If using a raised stage, the edges should be clearly marked with lights, glow tape or other clear demarcation.
- Safety crew ("pushers and catchers") should be positioned to assist entrants with their stage entry/exit and in case someone gets too close or, worse, stumbles from the edge of the stage.

Staging Large Costumes
Reiterating from the section on judging: a large costume is defined as a costume that exceeds or extends past the size of the costumer's normal body. Large costumes include designs such as form-fitted costumes with wings, a large suit of foam or thermoplastic armor, a mechanized battle mech or robot, or an immense dragon with puppetry. The Masquerade Director will need to make careful logistical decisions before the Masquerade and take potential risks, navigation, staging, and judging requirements into careful consideration.

Staging of large costumes can be a daunting task; If the following recommendations are incorporated into the Masquerade rules and entrant information (disseminated before the competition), it will be easier to accommodate large costumes.

The Director may wish to encourage entrants with large costumes to bring their own handler familiar with the specific requirements of their entry. It may also be necessary to bring the workmanship judges to the costume rather than bringing the costume to them. If the entrant has not brought a handler with them to help navigate the stage environment, a volunteer other than the one assigned to that costumer's group of entries (i.e. the den parent) should be assigned to them to ensure that they are accommodated appropriately and can enter and exit the stage area safely. Handlers can also assist with providing documentation to the judges or communicating answers if the costume impairs communication with the costumer.

Additional rehearsal time may be necessary to ensure that the entrant is able to accurately navigate the stage without assistance while wearing or otherwise manipulating a large costume. The Masquerade Director may decide that the costume can only be presented offstage to accommodate its size or to meet safety requirements.

Large costumes should not be disqualified simply because of their size, but should be displayed, presented, and judged appropriately in a way that ensures all participants, audience members, and judges are safe. If there is no way to present a costume safely to the audience within the physical/legal limits of a show, the costume should be barred. (For instance, a flying or floating costume using rotor or lighter-than-air technology might not be allowed because safety or facility liability limitations prevent it from being accepted for the show.)

Accessibility and Accommodation

Stages should be accessible to people with mobility difficulties. If possible, stage dimensions and access points should be available ahead of the Masquerade so that the costumer's individual needs may be determined and accommodated appropriately, based on the nature of their mobility and/or limitations of their costume (size, vision impediment, etc.).

It is good practice to allow costumers to explain their needs and then find a way to address them, rather than assume that a specific accommodation will work. Disabilities, like costumes, do not come with cookie-cutter solutions. The costumer will be the best judge of what will and will not work for them to access the stage safely.

Technical and Stage Crew

Though some Masquerades provide custom lighting cues, individualized soundtracks, and backdrop video projection to support the entries, a Masquerade does not require complicated and expensive theater tech.

Plan to publish the following tech specifications ahead of time if possible: The extent of the technical amenities for a Masquerade, and preferred audio format(s) (and video, if applicable), and method of delivery to the tech crew, as well as the level of stage crew/helpers who will be available to assist with entries' entrances, exits, and any prop or stage placement/removal.

Some entries may prefer to bring their own non-costumed crew, handlers or "stage ninjas" to assist them with their specific needs backstage or for their entry. Planning in advance to accommodate such helpers can make the show run more smoothly.

Green Room/Participant Lounge

The Green Room or Participant Lounge is a backstage/offstage area where the Masquerade entrants assemble before the show begins, and possibly where they wait while the judges deliberate.

An ideal Green Room has space for everyone and their props, with seating to accommodate them, drinking water, and access to restrooms for the entrants.

The Green Room should have a straightforward path to the location where entrants will enter the stage, ideally with a door that can muffle noise that might carry from the Green Room.

Most large ICG-style Masquerades organize the entries into "dens" of around 10-12 entrants in the Green Room, with a backstage volunteer ("den parent") to monitor them for problems and make sure they know when to get into line to go on stage. A den might comprise a single large group entry, or 8-10 solo entries.

A well-laid-out Green Room can also provide a space for the workmanship judges to examine the entries backstage.

Depending on the Masquerade's budget, entrants very much appreciate light non-messy snacks and a regularly refreshed water station. The staff should be sure to have straws available for entrants in complex makeup/masks/headgear.

The Green Room is also a good location for a small backstage costume repair station.

If the location is sufficiently spacious, the Official Photography station can be placed in the Green Room, as well.

Photography

Official Photography
Collecting a visual record of all the entries in a Masquerade makes it possible to create and maintain an archive of the event. Digital photography technology means that those images can be available almost immediately after the event.

Selecting a photographer with the skills and experience to cope with the wide variety of costumes they may encounter in front of their camera, and an assistant to help the costumers pose appropriately makes the process run more smoothly.

The best arrangement is to have an area set aside with adequate lighting and a good neutral background that each entry visits in turn as part of the flow of the Masquerade. An alternative is to have a photographer staged in the audience with a clear shot of the stage to capture each entry during its presentation. This will not capture the detail that photos taken in a dedicated photo area can achieve.

The technical specs for lighting and background will depend on budget, space, and available power in that space. A simple well-lit corner with a neutral wall can be adequate if budget is limited.

Fan Photography
Many attendees of a Masquerade will be interested in taking photographs of the entries, which the ICG refers to as Fan Photography.

If space permits, setting up an area with lighting and a neutral background for fan photographers as part of the traffic flow for an entry will be appreciated by those photographers. We recommend entries visit any fan photography area after they have finished their stage presentation. It is important to have at least one volunteer to "wrangle" the flow of contestants through fan photography so that all entries get through the process in a timely manner.

Regrettably, there have been incidents of inappropriate behavior on the part of some photographers in Fan Photography areas, and/or misuse of the images they have taken. Costumers should always have the option to opt out of posing for Fan Photography, and Masquerade Directors must be prepared to eject or bar photographers who fail to demonstrate proper restraint and respect for costumers.

An alternative to constructing a Fan Photography Area off stage is to bring the entries back out on stage while the judges deliberate so fans may shoot photos from the audience. This entails a different sort of wrangling to ensure that all the costumes get a turn in front of the cameras, and that the photographers all get an opportunity to shoot.

Photography from the Audience During the Show

The Masquerade Director may choose whether to permit available light photography from the audience during the actual entry presentations on stage. We note that almost every audience member now carries a high-resolution camera in their pocket via their smartphones, so banning all photography outright is unlikely to succeed.

Absolutely No Flash Photography should be permitted during the performance. Camera flashes can disorient the contestants, disrupt the lighting of the show, and even trigger seizures in sensitive individuals. For basic safety and comfort reasons, only available light photography should be permitted. The MC should announce this before the first costume enters the stage.

The Masquerade Director may choose whether to designate a specific area in the audience for photographers who wish to take less casual photos. If so, information on how to sign up for a space in that area must be published in advance. Reasonable restrictions on equipment and behavior to ensure said photography does not diminish the experience of the rest of the audience should be included in that information, and those restrictions enforced.

If recorded music is being played, licensing restrictions may limit the right to video record a show which includes such music. Those restrictions must be made clear to the audience to avoid fines and penalties. This is another reasonable announcement for the MC to make before the show begins.

Rehearsal

The Value of Tech Rehearsal

For a smoother, more successful Masquerade, schedule time for technical rehearsal if possible. A key purpose of the tech rehearsal is to assess the safety of whatever the entrants plan to do on stage during their presentation.

Tech rehearsals provide a vital opportunity for entries to work with the Masquerade Director, crew, and MC, to make sure everyone's needs are documented so they can be met during the show.

Tech rehearsals also provide the tech crew a chance to hear and test any media being used during the show for proper playback on the tech equipment.

The tech and stage crews should mark cues, and the MC should review each entry and mark correct pronunciations and timings as necessary.

Informal Rehearsal Space

Masquerade entries often include groups of costumers who have gathered for the first time at the event itself, or entrants who may not have had sufficient opportunity to practice movement in their entire costume with props. If the masquerade venue has an area which may be set aside for entrants to rehearse their presentations informally, then tech rehearsal can focus on cues and safety rather than blocking of individual entries.

This does require that the space be available for participants' use for quite some time, which must be figured into a larger event schedule as it is created. If function space is at a premium during the day, but might be made available early in the morning or later in the evening, consider those options.

Arrange a sign-up procedure by which entrants can reserve the space for blocks of time. The basic stage dimensions, entrances, and exits should be marked out on the floor of such a rehearsal space.

Access to power so entrants may play sound for such rehearsals is always appreciated; there is no need to provide more advanced technical support in the space. A location which offers some privacy to avoid early revelation of the entries' staging is always appreciated.

Pre-Curtain Review

In the event a full rehearsal is not possible, a review backstage can stand in for rehearsal to some degree. The MC can confirm with each entry before "curtain time" (when the show begins) pronunciations and cues are correct, and similarly confirm the entry's tech requirements. Even with rehearsal, a final brief review can be useful.

Run Order

Once registration of the field of entries for a Masquerade has closed, the Masquerade Director can determine the run order (order in which the entries will appear on stage). If the Masquerade Director has a well-designed entry form that gathers all pertinent information, it's not hard to set the running order once registration has closed and to tell tech and entrants at tech rehearsal what each entry's running order number will be..

While one can simply send entries across the stage in registration order or segregate them by Skill Division, with some effort on the run order, the Director can control the overall flow of the show and improve both the audience and participant experience dramatically.

In constructing a running order, a Masquerade Director should look for the strongest entry to close the show but the second strongest to open it and a third strong entry somewhere around the middle of the running order (if possible). The closing entry is to let the audience leave happy or impressed. The opening entry is to catch their interest from the start. The entry in the middle revives interest that may be flagging in a large field of entries.

Putting the Junior/Youth Division first gets the youngest entrants across the stage early and reduces the chance that they will run out of patience/enthusiasm while waiting their turn.

If there is an entry likely to be a great finale to the show, put that entry in the final position.

Avoid putting entries that portray the same character or theme one right after the other (especially if the entries are in different Skill Divisions).

Mix solo and group entries, simple vs complicated presentations, and mix different Skill Divisions in the run order. This will also give the Tech Crew some breathing space between complicated entries.

Mix dramatic, comedic, and simple walk-on style entries, if possible.

Masquerade Directors may feel that large costumes are best presented at the end of the Masquerade; however, it may be very difficult for the costumer to wear the costume through the entire contest. If this is the case, the costumer's handler (or a Masquerade volunteer) should be available to help the costumer remove pieces as necessary and then put them back on in advance of their appearance on stage to ensure the costumer's safety and wellbeing.

Reset/Re-Run of Entries

If equipment problems or crew errors interfere with the presentation of an entry, the Masquerade Director and crew should offer the entrants an opportunity to re-run their entry with corrected lighting and/or sound cues.

Licensing Recorded Media for Use in a Masquerade

The Need for Music Licensing

If recorded media (video and/or audio) will be used during the show, be sure the necessary licensing is in place for the event. In the US such performance licensing is available primarily via BMI and ASCAP; equivalent licensing is available in other regions.

- ASCAP: *https://www.ascap.com/help/ascap-licensing*
- BMI: *https://www.bmi.com/licensing/#licensetools*

The cost of such licenses depends on the audience size at the event; if budgeted in advance licensing is not normally prohibitively expensive. If a competition is part of a larger event, such licensing may already be in place for the entire event.

Creating a Video Archive of a Masquerade

A performance license does not grant automatic license to stream or post the performance publicly; that typically requires a more expensive and complicated sync license for all the tracks used in the show.

One may, however, record the show for archival purposes, and, depending on the membership structure of the event, provide copies of that archive to the artists participating in the show.

(Licensing and copyright laws vary around the world; the Masquerade Director must be sure to check the exact legal limitations applicable to their region.

ARCHIVING COMPETITIONS AND AWARDS

Maintaining Our History

The ICG Pat & Peggy Kennedy Memorial Archives is the ICG's permanent historical collection. The Archives include the largest existing collection of photographs, video, and paper ephemera record of the costuming art in relation to Science Fiction conventions. The ICG has an ongoing project to digitize as much of that content as possible. *https://www.costume.org/wp/pat-and-peggy-kennedy-memorial-archives-catalog/*

In addition to posting the recipients of awards, with photographs of the entries in costume, on the event's social media, website, and print media, all Masquerade Directors are encouraged to provide the ICG with a complete set of entries, awards, photos, and other ephemera, regardless of the scope of their Masquerade.

International Costumers' Guild Archives

Masquerades that publicly advertise their use of the ICG Guidelines are especially encouraged to submit photos and names of their participants, including any awards won, so that their Masquerade entries can be included in the International Costumers' Guild Pat and Peggy Kennedy Memorial Archives.

Email a complete list of all entrants and any awards received, with accompanying photos that identify the entry and/or participants, to the ICG Archivist or Corresponding Secretary [email addresses here]. If the Masquerade is a Costume-Con event, a separate set of archival materials should be delivered to the Costume-Con Archivist. (See the Costume-Con Constitution for details.)

Privacy Considerations for Archives

Participants can opt to be included in the archives under their cosplay name or pseudonym, but should use the same name when entering in multiple Masquerades. Participants may opt out of including their legal name, or may choose to be included only as the costume name for the sake of anonymity.

This is particularly recommended in the case of costumers under the age of legal majority. Publication of personal information should always be done in compliance with applicable privacy laws and regulations.

Any release forms included in the registration process for entrants should be maintained as part of the event's archive, especially those releases for use of their name/image.

If a costumer has changed their name, respect their wishes for which name(s) they want used for their entries in the archives.

Recordings for National Collections

The U.S. Library of Congress, and several other national collections around the world have determined that "Masquerade Costuming" is a unique art form worthy of archiving and preservation.

Providing a video record of the competition (especially for national- or international-scope Masquerades) with supporting information on entries and results will help preserve our often too-ephemeral creations for posterity. Additional Resources

The Kennedy Masquerade Compendium (1981) edited by Peggy Kennedy is the seminal volume on running Masquerade contests. The *Masquerade Handbook* edited by Janet Wilson Anderson is another early resource on the topic. Regrettably, both volumes are currently out of print.

The ICG and its chapters frequently publish articles on the art of Masquerade production.

Some articles may be found in back issues of *The International Costumer* Newsletter. (*https://www.costume.org/wp/the-inter national-costumer-newsletter/*)

Of particular note, the article "Running a Small Masquerade" was published in issues 4 and 5 of volume VI (2007) (*https://www.costume.org/wp/the-international-costumer-newsletter/ #2007*) or the author's website. (*https://www.twistedimage.com/ costume/articles/Running%20a%20small%20Masquerade .pdf*)

The Virtual Costumer, the quarterly magazine of the Silicon Web Costumers' Guild, has also published several articles on Masquerade production. Back issues may be found at *https:// siwcostumers.org/vc-contents.html*. Volume 14, issue 1 (2016) is dedicated entirely to "The Art of the Masquerade." (*https://www. siwcostumers.org/vc_contents.html#v14_i1*)

The Kennedy Masquerade Compendium (1981) edited by Peggy Kennedy is the seminal volume on running Masquerade contests. The *Masquerade Handbook* edited by Janet Wilson Anderson is another early resource on the topic. Regrettably, both volumes are currently out of print.

The ICG and its chapters frequently publish articles on the art of Masquerade production.

Some articles may be found in back issues of *The International Costumer* Newsletter. *(https://www.costume.org/wp/the-internat ional-costumer-newsletter/)*

Of particular note, the article "Running a Small Masquerade" was published in issues 4 and 5 of volume VI (2007) *(https://www.costume.org/wp/the-international-costumer-newsletter/ #2007)*. It is also available on the author's website. *(https:// www.twistedimage.com/costume/articles/Running%20a%20small %20Masquerade.pdf)*

The Virtual Costumer, the quarterly magazine of the Silicon Web Costumers' Guild, has also published several articles on Masquerade production. Back issues may be found at *https:// www.siwcostumers.org/vc_contents.html*. Volume 14, issue 1 (2016) is dedicated entirely to "The Art of the Masquerade." *(https:// www.siwcostumers.org/vc_contents.html#v14_i1)*

The International Costumers' Guild is developing a modern library of Masquerade related resources for costumers and Masquerade participants and organizers. This document is part of that project.

AFTERWORD

These Guidelines are intended to be a living document, subject to addition and revision as time goes on. If you have suggestions, comments, or questions, please address them to *guidelines@ costume.org* and we shall endeavor to address them

INDEX

A

B

C

R

S

T

V

Video Archive · *See* Recorded Media

W

Workmanship Judging · *See* Judging

www.ingramcontent.com/pod-product-compliance
Lightning Source LLC
Chambersburg PA
CBHW020344130626
46549CB00003B/1281